The Water Cycle

by David Smith

Illustrations by John Yates

Thomson Learning • New York

Books in the series

The Human Cycle
The Food Cycle
The Plant Cycle
The Water Cycle

Words printed in **bold** can be found in
the glossary on page 30.

First published in the
United States in 1993 by
Thomson Learning
115 Fifth Avenue
New York, NY 10003

First published in 1993 by
Wayland (Publishers) Ltd.

Cataloging-in-Publication Data applied for

ISBN: 1-56847-092-4

Printed in Italy

Contents

Water everywhere   4

Fresh water, salty water   6

Disappearing water   8

Gathering clouds   10

Cloudburst   13

Filling the rivers   16

A supply of fresh water   18

Water treatment   20

Water pollution   22

Return to the sea   24

Fast and slow cycles   26

The water cycle   28

Glossary   30

Further reading   31

Index   32

Water everywhere

ABOVE The blue area in this photograph is the Pacific Ocean. Look how much of Earth's surface it covers.

When water freezes, it turns into ice crystals. They can form beautiful lacelike patterns.

If you were an astronaut gazing down on Earth, the first thing you would notice is that most of Earth's surface is covered with water. In fact, water covers nearly three-quarters of our world's surface.

The next time you pour yourself a glass of water, watch carefully how the water moves. Water is a **liquid**. It can flow and take on the shape of any object that holds it.

Water can change. If it is cooled, it will freeze and turn into ice. Ice is a **solid**. Ice can be made in a freezer. Look at some ice cubes. Can they flow like water? Do they keep their own shape?

Most of the world's ice is found at the South Pole (Antarctica) and the North Pole (the Arctic). Some ice is also found at the top of high mountains where it is very cold.

If ice is warmed, it will melt. If water is warmed, it will change into **water vapor**. Water vapor is a **gas**. Gases will spread in all directions. You can see this happen when the water in a teakettle boils. The steam spreads out. Water vapor is all around us in the air.

Some of the water at the North and South poles is frozen in huge icebergs, like this. They may contain ice that has been frozen for thousands of years.

Fresh water, salty water

Like many plants and animals these fish must live in salt water.

2% Ice

1% Fresh water

97% Salt water

Imagine that this glass contains all the world's water. This shows just how little fresh water there is.

Most of the world's water is salty and is found in seas and oceans. Many plants and animals need to live in this **salt water** to survive.

This tree frog needs to keep its skin wet with fresh water to stay alive.

The water in our ponds, lakes, and rivers is called **fresh water**. Many plants and animals live in fresh water. Others need it to drink, just as we do. In fact, humans use more fresh water than any other animal.

Only a tiny part of the world's water is fresh water. It seems amazing that we have never run out.

The reason why there is enough is that nature recycles fresh water. This has been going on ever since water first formed on Earth more than four billion years ago. This recycling is called the **water cycle**.

Humans use huge amounts of fresh water every day, in all sorts of ways. Most swimming pools are filled with fresh water.

Disappearing water

The water cycle starts in the open seas. The sun shines on seawater, causing some of it to evaporate.

Our journey around the water cycle starts in the open seas. As the sun shines on the sea, the heat turns some of the water into tiny drops of vapor. The water vapor rises into the sky, carried upward by warm air. This process is called **evaporation**.

This part of the water cycle is very important. When seawater evaporates, all the salt that was in it gets left in the sea. This means that the water is fresh when it comes back to the earth as rain.

See for yourself

See for yourself how salt water evaporates in the sun, leaving salt behind.

You will need: table salt, a plastic saucer or dish, and a pencil.

1. Fill the plastic saucer with a cup of fresh water and a few teaspoons of salt.

2. Mark the level of the water in the dish.

3. Place the saucer on a sunny windowsill.

4. Mark the water level every day.

5. What happens to the water after a week? What happens to the salt?

Evaporation does not just happen over the sea. It happens anywhere there is water and sunshine. In sunny weather, rain puddles soon dry out. Even ponds and lakes dry up a little because of evaporation. Water also evaporates from plants and trees.

When wet laundry is hung out to dry, the water evaporates into the air.

Gathering clouds

As warm air carries water vapor upward, the air cools down. Cold air cannot hold as much water vapor as warm air, so eventually the water vapor turns back into liquid water. This change from water vapor to liquid water is called **condensation**. You can see this happening when water vapor in the air condenses on a cold window pane.

See for yourself

Water vapor condenses in cold air. Put a glass of water in a refrigerator for about two hours. When the glass is cold, take it out and watch what happens.

The air around the glass has cooled, so it must let go of the water vapor. The vapor condenses into drops of water on the sides of the glass.

The air is full of tiny particles of dust. When condensation occurs millions of tiny drops of water form around the dust, making clouds.

Look at the sky on different days and you will see different patterns of clouds. These patterns come from three main types of clouds: cirrus, stratus, and cumulus.

Cirrus clouds are thin and wispy. They are made of ice crystals and are found high above Earth's surface, where the air is very cold.

Note the wispy appearance of these cirrus clouds.

This photograph shows flat stratus clouds that look like fog and fluffy, tall cumulus clouds.

Stratus clouds can be seen in layers or sheets across the sky. They are found at lower levels above Earth than cirrus clouds. Stratus clouds often blot out the sun and the blue sky, bringing rain or drizzle.

Cumulus clouds look like fluffy balls of cotton. They have flat bottoms and are often seen dotted around the sky on sunny days.

Cloudburst

Inside a cloud, water drops bump into each other and join together to make larger drops. The larger drops grow too heavy for the cloud to hold, and they fall to Earth as rain.

It begins to rain when water drops in clouds grow too heavy for the cloud to hold.

Rain is only one of the ways in which the water cycle brings water back to the surface of Earth. Water may also fall as hail and snow. Hailstones are raindrops that have moved back up into a freezing cloud on rising **air currents**. The raindrops freeze into solid balls of ice and then fall as hail. Sometimes hailstones move up and down inside a cloud many times before falling. Each time they rise into the cloud, another layer of ice forms and they grow larger. The largest hailstone ever measured landed in Kansas in 1970. It was 7.5 inches across. Fortunately most hailstones are no bigger than a pea!

How rain is made

Raindrops start as tiny drops of water vapor.

Bigger drops are made as smaller ones join together.

Cross section of a hailstone

By slicing a hailstone in half and counting the layers of ice, a water scientist can tell how many times the hailstone rose back into the cloud.

How snowflakes are made

Snowflakes start as tiny wafers of ice.

The ice crystals attract one another and join together to make beautiful snowflakes. No two are alike.

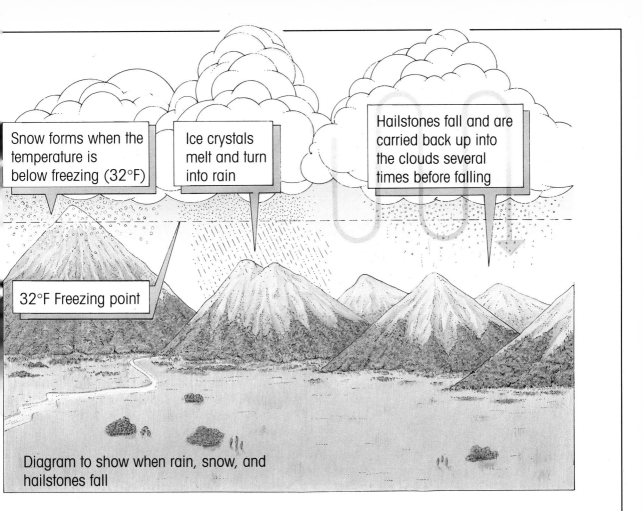

Snow forms when the temperature is below freezing (32°F)

Ice crystals melt and turn into rain

Hailstones fall and are carried back up into the clouds several times before falling

32°F Freezing point

Diagram to show when rain, snow, and hailstones fall

Snow falls from clouds that are made of ice crystals. Inside these clouds, the ice crystals grow into snowflakes by joining other crystals. Then, as long as the air temperature below the clouds is cold enough, the snowflakes fall to Earth. Often the temperature below the clouds is warmer and the snowflakes melt and turn to rain. If the snowflakes fall in a very cold place they never melt. The snow is pressed down into ice and stays there for thousands of years.

The delicate pattern of a snowflake is made when ice crystals join together.

Filling the rivers

When water has fallen as rain, snow, or hail, it continues its journey by running into the rivers. This is the next step along the water cycle. Water can find its way into the rivers in many ways.

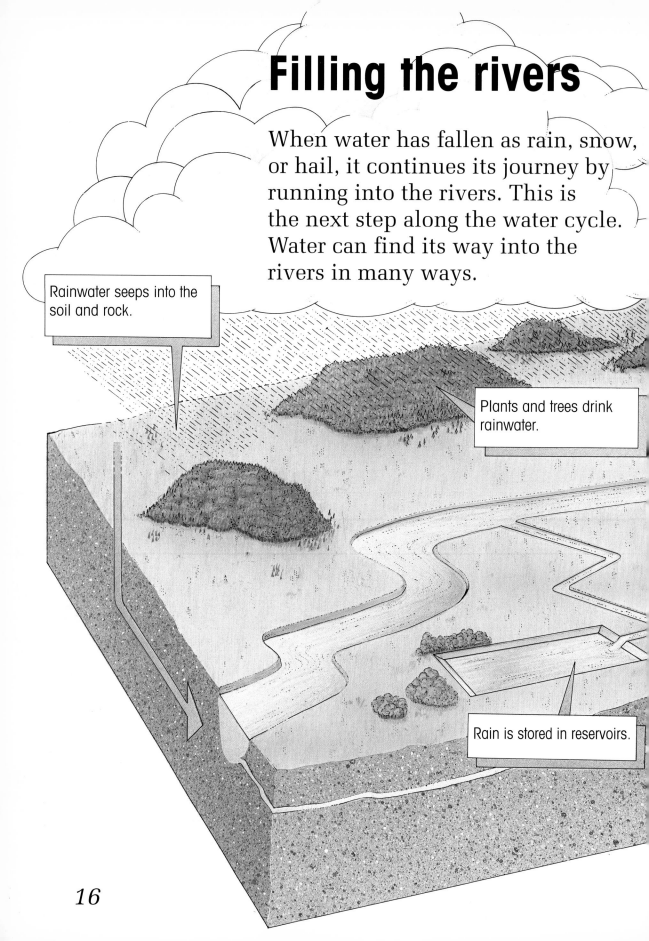

Rainwater seeps into the soil and rock.

Plants and trees drink rainwater.

Rain is stored in reservoirs.

Snow falls and is stored as ice.

Ice melts and finds its way into streams.

Streams join to make a river.

Rain is stored in ponds and lakes.

Rain flows over the ground and into streams.

Rain finds its way into underground rivers and lakes.

17

A supply of fresh water

Have you ever stopped to think how easy it is to turn on the faucet when you want fresh water?

The fresh water in our rivers can be used in many ways. Some water is taken out of our rivers and stored in **reservoirs**. Reservoirs are huge lakes that have been made to hold water. This water can be pumped to factories where is is used to cool down and clean machinery.

Fresh water is also pumped into our houses, schools, stores, and public buildings. We use this water for drinking, washing, and cooking, so it has to be very clean. For this reason the water is **treated** before it reaches our faucets. Leaves and dirt are removed by **filtering** the water through gravel beds. **Chlorine** is added to kill harmful germs. The people treating the water then make sure that it does not contain any dangerous chemicals.

When the water is clean and safe enough for us to use, it is pumped through underground pipes to where it is needed.

Farmers need a supply of fresh water for their animals to drink and to help their crops grow. It is not as important for this water to be treated, so farmers often take it straight from rivers, ponds, and underground wells.

This channel in France catches rainwater. Farmers use it to water their crops and animals can drink from it.

Water treatment

Dirty water is called **sewage**. Sewage travels in large underground pipes called sewers to treatment plants where it can be **recycled**.

When water has been used, it is dirty. Think of all the ways you can use water every day.

First the sewage passes through a large tank where big pieces of grit are removed. Next it is moved into a settling tank. The sewage stays there until all the tiny pieces in it have settled to the bottom of the tank to make **sludge**. The liquid sewage at the top of the settling tank is piped over a filter bed. There, air is bubbled through the sewage to help **bacteria** grow. The bacteria attack and kill germs.

Then the sewage is filtered through fine pebbles to take out any remaining grit.

The clean water that is produced by this treatment is called **effluent**. The effluent is now clean and safe enough to go back into rivers and continue its journey along the water cycle.

Gravel filter beds in a sewage plant are used to help clean dirty water.

See for yourself

See for yourself how to clean dirty water. You will need: muddy water, a coffee filter, gravel, sand, charcoal powder, and a plastic bottle.

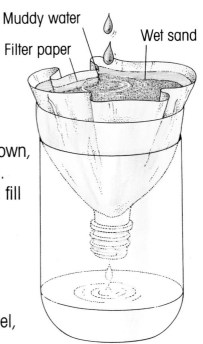

1. Cut the top off a plastic bottle, turn it upside down, and rest it on the remaining part of the bottle.
2. Place the coffee filter inside the bottle top and fill it with a layer of wet sand.
3. Pour the muddy water onto the sand.
4. Watch carefully as the water drips through. What do you notice?

See if you can improve your filter using the gravel, sand, and charcoal powder.

Water pollution

This photograph, taken under a microscope, shows the tiny creatures that live in all fresh water. Would you like to drink these?

In the natural **environment**, water is never as clean as when it comes out of our faucets. It is alive with tiny plants and animals. Look at the photograph on the left of mountain stream water. It was taken under a **microscope**. It shows that fresh water is full of living creatures so small we cannot see them with our naked eyes. These tiny living things are needed by larger plants and animals to survive.

But humans have found ways to remove these living things from drinking water—even though they are not considered **pollution**. Pollution is anything harmful in the water that nature did not put there. Pollution often harms plants and animals, and sometimes kills them.

Garbage dumped thoughtlessly into ponds and streams looks ugly and can be dangerous. Wastewater from farms, houses, and factories is sometimes not cleaned properly. It may put dangerous chemicals and sewage into rivers and lakes.

This poor bird is covered with oil. When oil is spilled in our seas, wildlife always suffers.

This kind of pollution can cause terrible damage to the environment.

Many chemicals that are useful are also harmful **pollutants**. The chemicals in dishwashing liquid do a great job on dirty dishes, but what happens when they get into the water cycle?

Dumping garbage in a pond not only looks ugly, it causes terrible damage to the plants and animals that live there.

See for yourself

See for yourself how dishwashing liquid pollutes fresh water. You will need: a tray of water, a paper clip, and some dishwashing liquid.

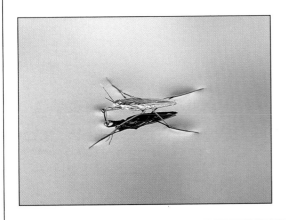

1. Place one paper clip carefully on the surface of the water so that it floats.

2. Now add a drop or two of dishwashing liquid. What happens? Can you find out why?

How might pollution by these chemicals affect the pond skater in this photograph?

A pond skater stands on the surface of the water.

Return to the sea

Cleaned and treated water returns to our rivers. All rivers eventually reach the sea, and the water in them finally completes the water cycle.

A river's journey starts high in the mountains. The river starts life as a small, fast stream that tumbles down the slopes of hills and mountains. At this stage the water in a mountain stream looks crystal clear.

Diagram to show a river's journey, from high in the mountains down to the sea.

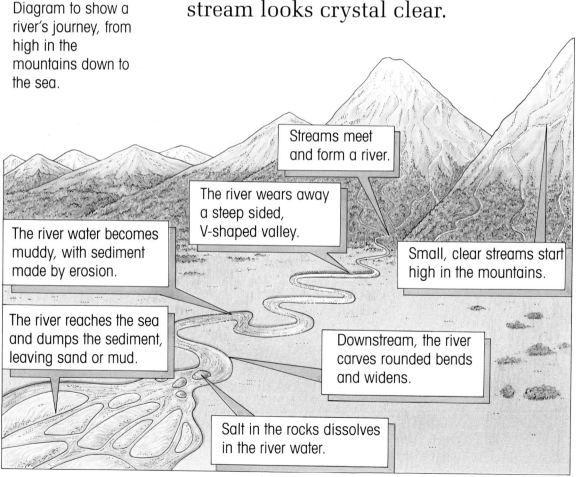

Streams meet and form a river.

The river wears away a steep sided, V-shaped valley.

The river water becomes muddy, with sediment made by erosion.

Small, clear streams start high in the mountains.

The river reaches the sea and dumps the sediment, leaving sand or mud.

Downstream, the river carves rounded bends and widens.

Salt in the rocks dissolves in the river water.

Mountain streams join together and widen into a river. The river carves a valley out of the land as it flows toward the sea.

Rivers make their valleys by **erosion**. The power of the water carries stones and rocks along the riverbed. These stones and rocks scrape away at the riverbed and eat into the banks. As the river flows to the sea, it gets wider and deeper. The water is now much muddier than it was because it is full of tiny particles picked up by erosion.

As the river flows over rock, it **dissolves** the salt in the rock. This small amount of salt in the fresh river water is carried out to sea. When the seawater evaporates, the salt is left behind in the sea and the water cycle starts again.

TOP A river begins high in the mountains, as a tumbling stream.

BELOW A river widens and deepens as it flows toward the sea.

Fast and slow cycles

Tropical rain forests get more than 100 inches of rain each year. Temperate climates, such as the eastern United States, get about 20 inches each year.

Tropical rain forests, found near the **equator**, have the fastest water cycle in the world. In these areas the whole water cycle happens in just one day.

It is always very hot in tropical rain forests. The heat causes a lot of water from the many plants in the forest to evaporate. The warm air holds a lot of water vapor. Eventually so much

evaporation takes place that the air cannot hold any more water. When this happens, a short, violent rainfall takes place.

Hot deserts have the slowest water cycle in the world. Sometimes it can take years before it rains in a hot desert.

The air over deserts is hot and dry during the day. It does not rise and cool down, but remains close to the ground, staying hot. Any water vapor in the air during the day cannot condense and form rain clouds. This lack of rainfall is called a drought.

Deserts receive very little rain each year. Some years they get no rain at all. Most plants and animals find it very difficult to live in deserts.

The water cycle

Cooler temperatures cause condensation and clouds to form.

The sun's rays warm the ocean and the land.

Water vapor is carried up by rising warm air.

Evaporation of water from plants and soil

Evaporation of water from the sea

The energy to drive the water cycle comes from the sun. Water changes from vapor, to liquid, to solid, and back to liquid again. This natural recycling of water is vital to the survival of all life on Earth.

Evaporation of water from lakes, ponds, and rivers

Glossary

Air currents Streams of air. If warm, they will rise.

Bacteria Tiny living things that are all around us. Some are harmful.

Chlorine A chemical added to water to kill harmful bacteria.

Condensation The changing of water vapor into liquid water as it cools.

Dissolves Melts into something. Salt dissolves in water.

Effluent Water produced after sewage is cleaned.

Environment Everything around us, including our houses, the countryside, towns, and buildings.

Equator An imaginary line running around the center of Earth. Temperatures are higher there.

Erosion The wearing away of land by water or wind.

Evaporation The changing of liquid water to water vapor, brought about by heat.

Filtering Passing water through sand and gravel to make it cleaner.

Fresh water Water that is not salty.

Gas An air-like substance that spreads into the whole of the space around it.

Liquid Anything that can flow, such as water.

Microscope An instrument that shows things too small to be seen with the naked eye.

Pollutants Things that cause pollution.

Pollution Damage to the environment caused by garbage and dangerous chemicals.

Recycled Made ready to be used again.

Reservoirs Lakes made to store fresh water for use by humans.

Salt water Water containing salt. Ocean water is salt water.

Sewage Wastewater from houses and factories.

Sludge A muddy substance that is made after sewage has settled.

Solid Any substance that has its own shape and does not flow. Wood is a solid.

Treat To change something in a way that makes it safe.

Tropical rain forests Thick forests with high rainfall that are found near the equator. They are full of many thousands of types of plants and animals.

Water cycle The natural process that recycles water.

Water vapor The gas into which water is changed by heat.

Further Reading

Davies, Kay and Wendy Oldfield. *The Super Science Book of Weather.* Super Science. New York: Thomson Learning, 1993.

Dickinson, Jane. *Wonders of Water.* Mahwah, NJ: Troll Associates, 1983.

Dorros, Arthur. *Follow the Water from Brook to Ocean.* New York: HarperCollins, 1991.

Richardson, Joy. *The Water Cycle.* Picture Science. New York: Franklin Watts, 1992.

Seed, Deborah. *Water Science.* Redding, Mass.: Addison-Wesley, 1992.

Taylor, Barbara. *Water at Work.* Science Starters. New York: Franklin Watts, 1991.

Picture acknowledgments

The publishers would like to thank the following for allowing their pictures to be reproduced in this book: Bruce Coleman 11 (J. Foott), 12 (top, J. Shaw), 25 (bottom, F. Prenzel); Environmental Picture Library 7 (top, P. Brown), 28 (M. Mckinnon); Zul Mukhida 9; Oxford Scientific Films 6 (L. Gould), 22 (top); Science Photo Library 4 (top, T. Vant Sant), 13 (A. Pasieka), 18 (S. Terry), 21 (M. Bond), 25 (top, Dr. M. Read); Tony Stone Worldwide (cover picture, center and background, bottom), 5, 6, (bottom), 8 (D. Bjorn), 15 (K. Hilsen), 24 (top, G. B. Lewis), 27 (P. Lamberti), Zefa 13, 19, 24, 26 (G. Braasch).

Index

air 10, 11
   currents 14
animals 6, 7, 18, 20

clouds 11, 12, 13, 14, 15,
   29
condensation 10, 11, 29

deserts 29

Earth 4, 11, 12, 13, 14, 15,
   28
effluent 21
equator 28
erosion 20, 25
evaporation 8, 9, 29

filtering 18
fresh water 6, 7, 8, 18, 22,
   25

hail 14, 16

ice 4, 5, 11, 15

lakes 7, 9, 18

North Pole (Arctic) 5

plants 6, 7, 9, 20
pollution 22, 23
ponds 7, 9, 19, 22

rain 9, 12, 13, 14, 15, 16
reservoirs 18
rivers 7, 16, 18, 19, 22, 24

salt 6, 8, 9, 25
sea 6, 8, 24, 25
sewage 20
snow 14, 15, 16
South Pole (Antarctica) 5,
   15
sunshine 8, 9, 12, 28

tropical rain forests 28, 29

water
   cycle 7, 14, 16, 20, 21
      24, 28, 29
   drops 8, 11, 13, 14
   vapor 5, 8, 10, 11, 25,
      29